DEEPENING
LIFE
TOGETHER

PARABLES

LIFE TOGETHER

BakerBooks
a division of Baker Publishing Group
Grand Rapids, Michigan

© 2009 by Lifetogether Publishing

Published by Baker Books
a division of Baker Publishing Group
P.O. Box 6287, Grand Rapids, MI 49516-6287
www.bakerbooks.com

Printed in the United States of America

Library of Congress Cataloging-in-Publication Data
Parables / [editors, Mark L. Strauss, Teresa Haymaker].
    p. cm. — (Deepening life together)
    Includes bibliographical references.
    ISBN 978-0-8010-6849-2 (pbk.)
    1. Jesus Christ—Parables—Textbooks. 2. Jesus Christ—Parables—Study and teaching.
I. Strauss, Mark L. II. Haymaker, Teresa.
BT375.3.P36 2009
226.80071—dc22   2009014249

CONTENTS

ACKNOWLEDGMENTS

The *Deepening Life Together: Parables* Small Group Video Bible Study has come together through the efforts of many at Baker Publishing Group, Lifetogether Publishing, and Lamplighter Media for which we express our heartfelt thanks.

Executive Producer	John Nill
Producer and Director	Sue Doc Ross
Editors	Mark L. Strauss (Scholar), Teresa Haymaker
Curriculum Development	Brett Eastman, Stephanie French, Teresa Haymaker, Pam Marotta, Leslye Miyashiro, Karen Lee-Thorp
Video Production	Chris Balish, Rodney Bissell, Nick Calabrese, Sebastian Hoppe Fuentes, Josh Greene, Patrick Griffin, Teresa Haymaker, Oziel Jabin Ibarra, Natali Ibarra, Janae Janik, Keith Sorrell, Lance Tracy
Teachers and Scholars	Mark Strauss, Joanne Jung, Daniel Watson
Baker Publishing Group	Jack Kuhatschek

Special thanks to DeLisa Ivy, Bethel Seminary, Talbot School of Theology, Wheaton College

READ ME FIRST

Most people want to live a healthy, balanced spiritual life, but few achieve this by themselves. And most small groups struggle to balance all of God's purposes in their meetings. Groups tend to overemphasize one of the five purposes, perhaps fellowship or discipleship. Rarely is there a healthy balance that includes evangelism, ministry, and worship. That's why we've included all of these elements in this study so you can live a healthy, balanced spiritual life over time.

A typical group session will include the following:

Memory Verses

For each session we have provided a memory verse that emphasizes an important truth from the session. This is an optional exercise, but we believe that memorizing Scripture can be a vital part of filling our minds with God's Word. We encourage you to give this important habit a try.

 CONNECTING *with God's Family (Fellowship)*

The foundation for spiritual growth is an intimate connection with God and his family. A few people who really know you and who earn your trust provide a place to experience the life Jesus invites you to live. This section of each session typically offers you two activities. You can get to know your whole group by using the icebreaker question, and/or you can check in with one or two group members—your spiritual partner(s)—for a deeper connection and encouragement in your spiritual journey.

DVD TEACHING SEGMENT. A *Deepening Life Together: Parables* Video Teaching DVD companion to this study guide is available. For each study session, the DVD contains a lesson taught by Mark Strauss. If you are using the DVD, you will view the teaching segment after your *Connecting* discussion and before your group discussion time (the *Growing* section). At the end of each session in this study guide, you will find space for your notes on the teaching segment.

GROWING *to Be Like Christ (Discipleship)*

Here is where you come face-to-face with Scripture. In core passages you'll explore what the Bible teaches about the topic of the study. The focus won't be on accumulating information but on how we should live in light of the Word of God. We want to help you apply the Scriptures practically, creatively, and from your heart as well as your head. At the end of the day, allowing the timeless truths from God's Word to transform our lives in Christ is our greatest aim.

DEVELOPING *Your Gifts to Serve Others (Ministry)*

Jesus trained his disciples to discover and develop their gifts to serve others. And God has designed each of us uniquely to serve him in a way no other person can. This section will help you discover and use your God-given design. It will also encourage your group to discover your unique design as a community. In this study, you'll put into practice what you've learned in the Bible study by taking a step to serve others. These simple steps will take your group on a faith journey that could change your lives forever.

SHARING *Your Life Mission Every Day (Evangelism)*

Many people skip over this aspect of the Christian life because it's scary, relationally awkward, or simply too much work for their busy schedules. But Jesus wanted all of his disciples to help outsiders connect with him, to know him personally. This doesn't mean preaching on street corners. It could mean welcoming a few newcomers into your group, hosting a short-term group in your home, or walking through this study with a friend. In this study, you'll have an opportunity to go beyond Bible study to biblical living.

SURRENDERING *Your Life for God's Pleasure (Worship)*

God is most pleased by a heart that is fully his. Each group session will give you a chance to surrender your heart to God in prayer and worship. You may read a psalm together, share a page in your journal, or sing a song to close your meeting. If you have never prayed aloud in a group before, no one will pressure you. Instead, you'll experience the support of others who are praying for you.

Study Notes

This section provides background notes on the Bible passage(s) you examine in the *Growing* section. You may want to refer to these notes during your group meeting or as a reference for those doing additional study.

For Deeper Study (Optional)

If you want to dig deeper into more Bible passages about the topic at hand, we've provided additional passages and questions. Your group may choose to do study homework ahead of each meeting in order to cover more biblical material. Or you as an individual may choose to study the *For Deeper Study* on your own. If you prefer not to do study homework, the *Growing* section will provide you with plenty to discuss within the group. These options allow individuals or the whole group to go deeper in their study, while still accommodating those who can't do homework or are new to your group.

You can record your discoveries in your journal. We encourage you to read some of your insights to a friend (spiritual partner) for accountability and support. Spiritual partners may check in each week over the phone, through e-mail, or at the beginning of the group meeting.

Reflections

On the *Reflections* pages we provide Scriptures to read and reflect on between group meetings. We suggest you use this section to seek God at home throughout the week. This time at home should begin and end with prayer. Don't get in a hurry; take enough time to hear God's direction.

Subgroup for Discussion and Prayer

If your group is large (more than seven people), we encourage you to separate into groups of two to four for discussion and prayer. This is to encourage greater participation and deeper discussion.

INTRODUCTION

Welcome to the *Deepening Life Together* Bible study on the *Parables*. As we live this Bible study experience together during the next four weeks, we will unpack a few of the parablesor stories—Jesus told that reveal the faithfulness of God. The journey will bring us to a greater understanding of God's love for his lost children and his desire that all return to him. As you read, discuss, and reflect on the topic of each session, your confidence in God's faithfulness will grow to new heights.

Jesus was a master storyteller. His parables—simple stories from everyday life—were entertaining yet contained a powerful spiritual message. The parables would lure people to listen and then catch them with powerful conviction in some area of spiritual need. Our first parents—Adam and Eve—compromised our relationship with God by a foolish ambition to be independent. Through these parables, Jesus reveals the nature of repentance and the Lord's readiness to welcome and bless all who return to him.

For some of you, this might be the first time you've connected in a small group community. We want you to know that God cares about you and your spiritual growth. As you prayerfully respond to the principles you learn in this study, God will move you to a deeper level of commitment and intimacy with himself, as well as with those in your small group.

We at Baker Books and Lifetogether Publishing look forward to hearing the stories of how God changes you from the inside out during this small group experience. We pray God blesses you with all he has planned for you through this journey together.

> For the LORD is good and his love endures forever;
> his faithfulness continues through all generations.

Psalm 100:5 (NIV)

PARABLE OF THE PRODIGAL SON

Memory Verse: "For this son of mine was dead and is alive again; he was lost and is found." So they began to celebrate (Luke 15:24 NIV).

Jesus associated with sinners because he wanted to bring the lost—people considered beyond hope—the gospel of God's kingdom. He sets forth the gospel of grace, encouraging everyone to repent and return to him.

In telling the parable of the prodigal son, Jesus spoke to tax collectors and sinners in the hearing of the Pharisees (Luke 15:1–2). The message was for all of them.

If you feel far from God, don't despair. He is searching for you.

Connecting

Open your group with prayer. Ask God to prepare your hearts to receive his Word through this Bible study and for the courage to respond as he challenges you in the weeks to come.

Deeper relationships happen when we take the time to keep in frequent touch with one another. As you begin, pass around a copy of the *Small Group Roster*, a sheet of paper, or one of you pass your study guide, opened to the *Small Group Roster*. When the roster gets to you, write down your contact information, including the best time and method for contacting you. Then, someone volunteer to make copies or type up a list with everyone's information and e-mail it to the group this week.

1. Begin this first session by introducing yourselves. Include your name, what you do for a living, and what you do for fun. You may also include whether or not you are married, how long you have been married, how many children you have, and their ages. Also share what brought you to this *Deepening Life Together: Parables* small group study and what you expect to learn during the next four weeks.

2. Talk about a time when you lost a child in a public place or you were separated from your family or friends in an unfamiliar place. How did you feel?

3. Whether your group is new or ongoing, it's always important to reflect on and review your group values. In the *Appendix* is a *Small Group Agreement* with the values we've found most useful in sustaining healthy, balanced groups. We recommend that you review these values and choose one or two—values you haven't previously focused on or have room to grow in—to emphasize during this study. Choose values that will take your group to the next stage of intimacy and spiritual health.

 Growing

Three lost-and-found stories are found in Luke, beginning in verse 15:4. In all the stories the message is the same: the loss causes extraordinary pain and a longing for that which is lost, and the finding leads to extraordinary joy. The main theme of the three parables is God's great joy in the salvation of the lost. The third one—the parable of the lost son—is perhaps the most famous parable Jesus told.

Jesus spoke to to the least respectable Jews in his society in the hearing of some of the most devout, the Pharisees (Luke 15:1–2). Read Luke 15:11–32 aloud.

4. In Jewish society it was rare for a man to distribute his inheritance while he was still alive. Even more shocking is that the younger son asked that this be done (v. 12), because respect for parents was a strong social value. What do you think might have prompted the son to ask for his inheritance? What clue do you get from verse 13 about the son's motives?

Who in your life, or in our world, does the younger son remind you of? Why?

5. How do you think the father might have felt about his son's decisions?

Why do you think the father agreed to the son's request?

6. Have you ever felt the need to escape, or have you ever known anyone to do this? What kinds of things precipitated it? What were the results?

How do you think God views such actions?

7. Our decisions frequently affect our relationships with those closest to us. What effect do you think the son's rejection of his father (v. 14) had on their relationship?

How do you think this relates to our relationship with our heavenly Father?

8. Pig meat was unclean for Jews to eat (Deut. 14:8), and pagans had even persecuted Jews by forcing them to eat pork, so for Jews, pigs represented paganism. What does Luke 15:15 say about the condition of the younger son at this point in the story?

9. The son finally came to his senses and decided to return home. What does verse 17 say about the son's initial reasons for returning home? What does verse 19 say about his expectations once he arrived there?

10. How does verse 20 communicate what the father had been going through while his son was gone?

What do the father's actions say about his feelings for his son?

11. Talk about the significance of the robe, ring, sandals, and fine feast the father bestowed on the son in verses 22–24. What do you think the father was saying with these gifts? See the *Study Notes* for help.

12. When the older brother came home from working in the field and found his household celebrating the return of his prodigal brother, he was angry (v. 28). Why do you think that the older brother could not accept his brother's return as his father did?

13. What do you learn about the older brother's character from verses 28–30? For instance, how would you assess his level of obedience to his father?

14. "My son," the father said, "you are always with me, and everything I have is yours" (Luke 15:31 NIV).

What is Jesus saying here to the "older brothers" among us?

15. Verse 32 is an invitation to the Father's joy. With which character in the story—the younger brother, the older brother, or the father—do you most identify? Why?

God's love is never-ending, patient, and welcoming. He will reach out to us and give us opportunities to respond, but he will not force us to come to him. Like the father in this parable, God waits patiently for us to come to our senses.

 Developing

God has given every believer special gifts to be used for serving him and the body of Christ as the Holy Spirit leads. As we strive to deepen our relationship with him through his Word, prayer, and reflection, we learn to recognize the leading of the Holy Spirit.

16. One important way to discover and develop our God-given design is to partner with another Christian for spiritual connection and accountability. We call this a spiritual partnership.

    We strongly recommend each of you partner with someone in the group to help you in your spiritual journey during this study. This person will be your spiritual partner for the next several weeks. He or she doesn't have to be your best friend, but will simply encourage you to complete the goals you set for yourself during this study. Following through on a resolution is tough when you're on your own, but we've found it makes all the difference to have a partner cheering us on. In the *Appendix* we've provided a *Personal Health Plan*, a chart for keeping track of your spiritual progress. You and your spiritual partner can use it for accountability to the goals you set for yourselves. See the *Leader's Notes* for instructions for establishing spiritual partners and for beginning to use the *Personal Health Plan*.

Sharing

Jesus encouraged us to share his love and concern for the lost. As in the story of the prodigal son, the Father deals with human beings with a will of their own, but he is ready to greet his children if they choose to return to him. How can we help? We can take one of the small steps suggested below in the *Circles of Life* exercise.

17. Use the *Circles of Life* diagram (next page) to help you think of people you come in contact with on a regular basis who need to be connected in Christian community. Try to write two names in each circle. Consider the following ideas for reaching out to one or two of the people you list and make a plan to follow through with them this week.

    ☐ This is a wonderful time to welcome a few friends into your group. Which of the people on your list could you

15

invite? It's possible that you may need to help your friend overcome obstacles to coming to a place where he or she can encounter Jesus. Does your friend need a ride to the group or help with child care?

☐ Consider inviting a friend to attend a weekend church service with you and possibly plan to enjoy a meal together afterward. This can be a great opportunity to talk with someone about your faith in Jesus.

☐ Is there someone who is unable to attend your group but who still needs a connection? Would you be willing to have lunch or coffee with that person, catch up on life, and share something you've learned from this study? Jesus doesn't call all of us to lead small groups, but he does call every disciple to spiritually multiply his or her life over time.

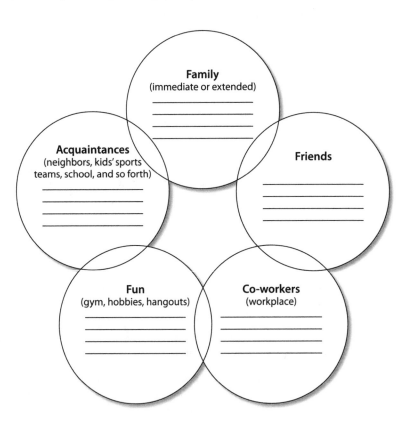

Surrendering

God is most pleased by a heart that is fully his. Each group session will provide group members an opportunity to surrender their hearts to God in prayer and worship.

18. Every believer should have a plan for spending time alone with God. At the end of each session, we have provided *Reflections* for you to begin daily time with him. There are five daily Scripture readings with room to record your thoughts. These will offer reinforcement of the principles we are learning and help you develop the habit of time alone with God throughout the week.

19. Before you close your group in prayer, answer this question: "How can we pray for you this week?" Write prayer requests on your *Prayer and Praise Report* and commit to praying for each other throughout the week.

20. The *Deepening Life Together: Parables* Video Teaching DVD companion for this study includes worship sets for use during your study. Choose one of these to end your study today.

Study Notes

Prodigal: A prodigal is one who is rashly or wastefully extravagant.

Inheritance, the Right of the Firstborn: The Mosaic law regulated the succession to real property as follows: it has to be divided among the sons, the eldest receiving a double portion, the others equal shares; if there were no sons, it went to the daughters, on the condition that they did not marry out of their own tribe. If there were no daughters, it went to the brother of the deceased; if no brother, to the paternal uncle; and, failing these, to the next of kin.

Feeding the Pigs: Pigs were considered unclean to the Jews—this would have been the most degrading work.

Pods: Seeds of the carob tree that are virtually indigestible by humans.

Best Robe, Ring, Sandals, Feast: These were all signs of position and acceptance. The robe signifies distinction; the ring, authority; the sandals, a member of the family for slaves went barefoot; the feast, to celebrate a special occasion.

For Deeper Study (Optional)

Read each passage below and consider what the passage says about the questions that follow:

> We all, like sheep, have gone astray, each of us has turned to his own way; and the LORD has laid on him the iniquity of us all. He was oppressed and afflicted, yet he did not open his mouth; he was led like a lamb to the slaughter, and as a sheep before her shearers is silent, so he did not open his mouth. By oppression and judgment he was taken away. And who can speak of his descendants? For he was cut off from the land of the living; for the transgression of my people he was stricken. He was assigned a grave with the wicked, and with the rich in his death, though he had done no violence, nor was any deceit in his mouth. Yet it was the LORD's will to crush him and cause him to suffer, and though the LORD makes his life a guilt offering, he will see his offspring and prolong his days, and the will of the LORD will prosper in his hand. After the suffering of his soul, he will see the light [of life] and be satisfied; by his knowledge my righteous servant will justify many, and he will bear their iniquities. Therefore I will give him a portion among the great, and he will divide the spoils with the strong, because he poured out his life unto death, and was numbered with the transgressors. For he bore the sin of many, and made intercession for the transgressors (Isa. 53:6–12 NIV).

- Isaiah speaks of Israel straying from God and compares them to wandering sheep. What does this say about the human condition?
- Who is "he" who is spoken of in verses 7 and following? What is "his" role in our salvation?
- What does verse 12b, "For he bore the sin of many, and made intercession for the transgressors," indicate about how this salvation comes about?

Therefore Jesus said again, "I tell you the truth, I am the gate for the sheep. All who ever came before me were thieves and robbers, but the sheep did not listen to them. I am the gate; whoever enters through me will be saved. He will come in and go out, and find pasture. The thief comes only to steal and kill and destroy; I have come that they may have life, and have it to the full. I am the good shepherd. The good shepherd lays down his life for the sheep" (John 10:7–11 NIV).

- Have you given your life to Jesus Christ, the "good shepherd," or are you still a wandering sheep?

Reflections

Each day, read the daily verses and give prayerful consideration to what you learn about God, his Spirit, and his place in your life. Then record your thoughts, insights, or prayer in the *Reflect* section below the verses you read. On the sixth day record a summary of what you have learned over the entire week through this study.

Day 1. Whoever loves skillful and godly Wisdom rejoices his father, but he who associates with harlots wastes his substance (Prov. 29:3 AMP).

REFLECT

_____

_____

_____

_____

Day 2. When he came to his senses, he said, "How many of my father's hired men have food to spare, and here I am starving to death! I will set out and go back to my father and say to him: Father, I have sinned against heaven and against you" (Luke 15:17–18 NIV).

REFLECT

_____

_____

_____

_____

Day 3. I tell you that in the same way there will be more rejoicing in heaven over one sinner who repents than over ninety-nine righteous persons who do not need to repent (Luke 15:7 NIV).

REFLECT

_____

_____

_____

_____

Day 4. The angel said to those who were standing before him, "Take off his filthy clothes." Then he said to Joshua, "See, I have taken away your sin, and I will put rich garments on you" (Zech. 3:4 NIV).

REFLECT

_____

_____

_____

_____

Day 5. "For this son of mine was dead and is alive again; he was lost and is found." So they began to celebrate (Luke 15:24 NIV).

REFLECT

_____
_____
_____
_____

Day 6. Use the following space to write any thoughts God has put in your heart and mind about the things we have looked at in this session and during your *Reflections* time this week.

SUMMARY

_____
_____
_____
_____

THE PHARISEE AND THE TAX COLLECTOR

Memory Verse: For everyone who exalts himself will be humbled, and he who humbles himself will be exalted (Luke 18:14b NIV).

The prayers of adults aren't always as honest or candid as they should be. In Luke 18, we find a parable about prayer and the attitude with which we should approach God.

 Connecting

Open your group with prayer. Pray that God would revive each group member's prayer life according to his Word, his righteousness, and his loving-kindness. Pray for continual strength to rejoice in God alone, seeking his face and will as we study about prayer today.

1. Think about the last time you prayed with a group of people outside of your small group. What strikes you as sincere about people's prayers? What strikes you as insincere? Talk about the characteristics of sincere God-directed prayer.

2. Sit with your spiritual partner. If your partner is absent or if you are new to the group, join with another pair or someone who doesn't yet have a partner. (If you haven't established your spiritual partnerships yet, turn to the *Session One Leader's Notes* in the *Appendix* for information on how to begin your partnerships.)

Turn to your *Personal Health Plan*. Share with your partner how your time with God went this week. What is one thing you discovered? Did you make a commitment to a next step that you can share? Make a note about your partner's progress and how you can pray for him or her.

Growing

After encouraging the disciples to be persistent in prayer (18:1–8), Jesus used a parable to teach them how to pray. This parable sharply contrasts the prayer of a Pharisee with that of a tax collector.

Read Luke 18:9–14 aloud.

3. To whom do you think Jesus spoke this parable? See verse 9 and the *Study Notes*.

   What might confidence in one's own righteousness look like today?

4. The two men in this story were as different as could be: One was scrupulous about practicing his religion, and the other was a moral disaster (see the *Study Notes* for more information on the Pharisee and tax collector). What does verse 10 suggest about mankind's access to God?

5. Read through Luke 18:11–12 using the table below. Discuss what each segment says about the Pharisee. How is the Pharisee's personality and self-assessment revealed through his prayer?

23

Verse (NIV)	What this says about the Pharisee
The Pharisee stood up and prayed about himself:	
"God, I thank you that	
I am not like other men—robbers, evil-doers, adulterers—or even like this tax collector.	
I fast twice a week and give a tenth of all I get."	

6. Read through Luke 18:13 using the table below. Discuss what each segment of the verse says about the tax collector. How is the tax collector's personality and self-assessment revealed through his prayer?

Verse (NIV)	What this says about the tax collector
But the tax collector stood at a distance.	
He would not even look up to heaven,	
but beat his breast and said, "God, have mercy on me, a sinner."	

7. Verse 18:14a says, "I tell you that this man, rather than the other, went home justified before God." See the *Study Notes* on what it means to be justified. Why did God judge the tax collector to be in a right relationship with God?

Why did God judge the Pharisee to be in a broken relationship with God?

8. Read Proverbs 28:13 below. How does this verse help us understand Luke 18:14?

He who conceals his sins does not prosper, but whoever confesses and renounces them finds mercy (NIV).

9. "For everyone who exalts himself will be humbled, and he who humbles himself will be exalted" (Luke 18:14b NIV). Why do you suppose humility is so essential in God's eyes?

10. What is God saying to you about prayer through this parable?

It's important to pray, but the attitude of prayer is vitally important. We can't impress God with our churchiness. God wants us to admit what is true about us and about him so that he can forgive us and draw us close. The proud will be humbled, but the humble will be honored and justified.

Developing

Jesus trained his disciples to discover and develop their gifts to serve others. And God has designed each of us uniquely to serve him in a way no other person can.

11. Is there an area of service that God has put on your heart to serve your small group or the body of Christ in your local church? Commit to taking the first step and be willing to let God lead you to the ministry that expresses your passion. In your *Personal Health Plan*, next to the "Develop" icon, answer the WHERE question: "WHERE are you serving?" If you are not currently serving, note one area where you will consider serving.

Sharing

Jesus wanted all of his disciples to help outsiders connect with him, to know him personally. Your small group can help you do this collectively and individually.

12. Return to the *Circles of Life* and review the names of those you chose to invite to this group, to church, or for one-on-one discipleship. How did it go? Share how your invitations went. If you are attending this group for the first time because someone invited you, feel free to share your perspective on this question.

If you haven't followed through, think about what is preventing you from doing so. As a group, consider some ways to overcome obstacles or excuses that keep us from reaching out and inviting people into our Christian community.

 Surrendering

We have learned in this session that our prayers reveal the condition of our hearts toward God.

13. Spend some time now surrendering your hearts to God through prayer and worship. Here are two ideas:

    ☐ Read a passage of Scripture aloud, giving God praise. You can have different people read a verse or a phrase. Consider using Psalm 147 for this exercise or choose one of your favorite passages. The point of this exercise is to focus on God and praise him for who he is and for what he does.

    ☐ Take turns in your group completing this sentence: Lord, I praise you for . . .

14. Share your prayer requests in your group and then gather in smaller circles of three or four people to pray. Be sure to write down the personal requests of the members to use as a reminder to pray for your group throughout the week. Then pray for one another in your circle.

Study Notes

Pharisees Were Confident of Their Own Righteousness: The people who were *confident of their own righteousness* were the Pharisees and other religious leaders who saw themselves as the only ones righteous enough to be acceptable to God. In Jesus's day the Pharisees were the most respected religious leaders. They not only obeyed the law of Moses, but had also accumulated a whole body of additional rules known as the "traditions of the elders." These traditions, not stipulated in Scripture, came from a desire to please God and avoid godless ways. But the Pharisee in the parable measures his worth by how well he met the standard—by what he is (not like other men), does (fasting twice a week), and gives (tithes). This made the Pharisees "confident in their own righteousness."

Tax Collector: Tax collectors were hated by their fellow Jews. They worked for the Romans and were viewed as traitors. They were also notoriously dishonest. They often assessed more taxes than were due. Tax collectors were considered the scum of the earth.

Justified: To be "justified" is to be declared forgiven of our sin by God. Our guilt is removed by the death of Jesus Christ as payment for our sin.

For Deeper Study (Optional)

Read Luke 18:1–8 below.

Then Jesus told his disciples a parable to show them that they should always pray and not give up. He said: "In a certain town there was a judge who neither feared God nor cared about men. And there was a widow in that town who kept coming to him with the plea, 'Grant me justice against my adversary.' For some time he refused. But finally he said to himself, 'Even though I don't fear God or care about men, yet because this widow keeps bothering me, I will see that she gets justice, so that she won't eventually wear me out with her coming!'" And the Lord said, "Listen to what the unjust judge says. And will not God bring about justice for his chosen ones, who cry out to him day and night? Will he keep putting them off? I tell you, he will see that they get justice, and quickly. However, when the Son of Man comes, will he find faith on the earth?" (NIV).

• What does this passage say to you about the value of persistence? How might this be applied to prayer?

Reflections

Each day, read the daily verses and give prayerful consideration to what you learn about God, his Spirit, and his place in your life. Then record your thoughts, insights, or prayer in the Reflect section below the verses you read. On the sixth day record a summary of what you have learned over the entire week through this study.

Day 1. He said to them, "You are the ones who justify yourselves in the eyes of men, but God knows your hearts. What is highly valued among men is detestable in God's sight" (Luke 16:15 NIV).

REFLECT

_____

_____

_____

_____

Day 2. And when you pray, do not be like the hypocrites, for they love to pray standing in the synagogues and on the street corners to be seen by men. I tell you the truth, they have received their reward in full (Matt. 6:5 NIV).

REFLECT

_____

_____

_____

_____

Day 3. Woe to you Pharisees, because you give God a tenth of your mint, rue and all other kinds of garden herbs, but you neglect justice and the love of God. You should have practiced the latter without leaving the former undone (Luke 11:42 NIV).

REFLECT

_____

_____

_____

_____

Day 4. O my God, I am too ashamed and disgraced to lift up my face to you, my God, because our sins are higher than our heads and our guilt has reached to the heavens (Ezra 9:6 NIV).

REFLECT

_____

_____

_____

_____

Day 5. For whoever exalts himself will be humbled, and whoever humbles himself will be exalted (Matt. 23:12 NIV).

REFLECT

_____

_____

_____

_____

Day 6. Use the following space to write any thoughts God has put in your heart and mind about the things we have looked at in this session and during your *Reflections* time this week.

SUMMARY

_____

_____

_____

_____

THE GREAT BANQUET

Memory Verse: God saved you by his grace when you believed. And you can't take credit for this; it is a gift from God (Eph. 2:8 NLT).

If God threw a party, would you drop everything to attend? Many Jews of Jesus's day were eagerly awaiting the feast that (according to prophecy) would come when the Messiah set everything right in Israel and ushered in the kingdom of God. But then came Jesus. He announced that the kingdom was at hand, but his teaching on the kingdom made many of the leading members of society uncomfortable. Some future after-you-die-and-go-to-heaven party is one thing, but dropping things here and now to follow Jesus in the hope that the party he promises will really happen—that's something else.

 Connecting

Open your group with prayer. Invite the Holy Spirit to draw you closer as a group.

1. Check in with your spiritual partner, or with another partner if yours is absent. Talk about any challenges you are currently facing in reaching the goals you set during this study. Tell your spiritual partner how he or she has helped you follow through with each step. Be sure to write down your partner's progress.

2. Begin to talk about what's next for your group. Do you want to continue meeting together? If so, the *Small Group Agreement* can help you talk through any changes you might want to make as you move forward. Consider what will you study, who will lead, and where and when you will meet.

Growing

Jesus was dining in the house of a prominent Pharisee (14:1). He had just finished talking about how unselfish servants will have blessing and repayment at the resurrection of the righteous. Someone who heard him say this said "Blessed is the man who will eat at the feast in the kingdom of God" (14:15 NIV). Like the people in last week's parable who were confident of their own righteousness (18:9), this speaker assumed he would share in the kingdom of God. As a Jew, he counted on his ancestry to reserve a place for him. In reply, Jesus told the parable of the great banquet.

Read Luke 14:15–24 aloud.

3. A master, who represents God, invites many guests to a great banquet. Initially they accept the invitations. Who do you think the invited guests represent? What does the invitation represent?

4. When the banquet is ready, the master sends his servant out to bring the guests in, but they suddenly make excuses and refuse to come. What kinds of things prevent the invited guests from accepting the master's invitation?

5. Jesus is the servant whom the Father sent into the world with his great invitation. From what you've read in earlier parables about the Pharisees and other leading men in Israel at that time, why did they reject his invitation?

6. The master is angry at the invited guests' excuses (v. 21). According to verses 21–24, what is the result?

What point do you think Jesus is making in this shocking turn of events?

7. The fact that the banquet hall is not filled even with the lowest classes of Jews causes the master to send the servants out again (14:23). Why do you think it is important to the master that the banquet hall be full?

Who do you think this additional guest list includes?

8. In the time of Jesus, who would have been the ultimate outsiders?

9. This parable was a stern warning to the Jews of Jesus's day. What does it say to us?

The banquet was a symbol of God's abundant blessing of salvation. Most of Israel rejected the invitation. Several decades later, the Jews of Judea rebelled against their Roman oppressors, and the Romans destroyed Jerusalem and its Jewish temple in AD 70. For Luke's readers, who lived shortly after that disaster, it was a potent warning to anyone who failed to take the invitation to God's banquet seriously.

The parable teaches us that while those originally invited (Israel's religious elite) rejected the invitation, the outsiders (poor, crippled, blind, lame, and Gentiles) who accept do receive God's salvation. It is God's grace alone and not who we are that allows us to enter his kingdom. We have the choice to refuse his invitation or humbly accept the gift that it is. Ultimately, we will be accountable for that decision. Will you joyfully come to the banquet, or will you foolishly make excuses?

Developing

Developing our ability to serve God and others according to the leading of the Holy Spirit takes time and persistence in getting to know our Lord. We must take time in prayer, in God's Word, and in meditation, to let God speak to us daily.

10. Commit to taking the necessary steps to grow closer to God by beginning one of the following habits this week.

☐ **Prayer.** Commit to personal prayer and daily connection with God. You may find it helpful to write your prayers in a journal.

☐ **Reflection.** Below is an opportunity for reading a short Bible passage five days a week. You also have the opportunity to write down your insights there. On the sixth day you can summarize what God has shown you throughout the week.

☐ **Meditation.** Try meditation as a way of internalizing God's Word more deeply. Copy a portion of Scripture on a card and tape it somewhere in your line of sight, such as your car's dashboard or the kitchen table. Think about it when you sit at red lights, or while you're eating a meal. Reflect on what God is saying to you through his words. Several passages for meditation are suggested on the *Reflections* pages in each session.

Sharing

One of the most loving acts a Christian can ever do is to share his or her faith with another person.

11. Return to the *Circles of Life* diagram and identify one or two people in each area of your life who need to know Christ. Write their names outside the circles for this exercise. Commit to praying for God's guidance and an opportunity to share with each of them.

12. Inviting people to church or Bible study is one way that we shepherd others toward faith in Christ. On your *Personal Health*

Plan, next to the "Sharing" icon, answer the "WHEN are you shepherding another person in Christ?" question.

13. If you have never invited Jesus to take control of your life, why not ask him in now? If you are not clear about God's gift of eternal life for everyone who believes in Jesus and how to receive this gift, take a minute to pray and ask God to help you understand what he wants you to do about trusting in Jesus.

 Surrendering

14. Share your praises and prayer requests with one another. Record these on the *Prayer and Praise Report*.

Study Notes

Banquet: A Middle Eastern banquet was a huge social affair. It was customary to first announce the event and then begin preparations based on the response. Preparations for the banquet would take many hours or days. It would be an enormous affront to the host to make excuses when the day came.

Elite Guests: The elite guests represent the religious leaders of Israel. When the people of Israel rejected God's salvation message, the nation experienced the destruction of Jerusalem and the temple in AD 70.

Messianic Banquet: At this banquet will be all those who have trusted Christ for salvation (see Isa. 25:6–7); they will come from every nation. Jesus had stated, "I tell you this, that many Gentiles will come from all over the world . . . and sit down with Abraham, Isaac, and Jacob at the feast in the Kingdom of Heaven" (Matt. 8:11 NLT).

For Deeper Study (Optional)

The great banquet parable is also told in Matthew 22:1–14, but with an added emphasis.

The Guest with Unworthy Clothes:

- In another surprising turn, one of the wedding guests does not have on proper attire, and so is thrown out of the banquet into the darkness, where there will be weeping and gnashing of teeth.
- The implication is that for these new guests, who would have nothing to wear to such a grand affair, the king has provided appropriate wedding garments. But this man refused to wear them.
- The application is that those who accept God's invitation to salvation cannot enter with their own "clothes," representing their sinful selves, but must put on God's righteous garments, representing the righteousness of God provided through Christ's life, death, and resurrection. Eternal destruction awaits those who think they can achieve salvation through their own works or worth.

What "improper clothes" do we try to wear as we join God's feast?

Reflections

Each day, read the daily verses and give prayerful consideration to what you learn about God, his Spirit, and his place in your life. Then record your thoughts, insights, or prayer in the Reflect section below the verses you read. On the sixth day record a summary of what you have learned over the entire week through this study.

Day 1. So just as sin ruled over all people and brought them to death, now God's wonderful grace rules instead, giving us right standing with God and resulting in eternal life through Jesus Christ our Lord (Rom. 5:21 NLT).

REFLECT

_____

_____

_____

_____

Day 2. By God's grace and mighty power, I have been given the privilege of serving him by spreading this Good News (Eph. 3:7 NLT).

REFLECT

_____

_____

_____

_____

Day 3. This same Good News that came to you is going out all over the world. It is bearing fruit everywhere by changing lives, just as it changed your lives from the day you first heard and understood the truth about God's wonderful grace (Col. 1:6 NLT).

REFLECT

_____

_____

_____

_____

Day 4. We are witnesses of these things, and so is the Holy Spirit, whom God has given to those who obey him (Acts 5:32 NIV).

REFLECT

_____

_____

_____

_____

Day 5. For by grace you have been saved through faith; and that not of yourselves, it is the gift of God (Eph. 2:8 NASB).

REFLECT

_____

_____

_____

_____

Day 6. Use the following space to write any thoughts God has put in your heart and mind about the things we have looked at in this session and during your *Reflections* time this week.

SUMMARY

_____

_____

_____

_____

THE GOOD SAMARITAN

Memory Verse: "Which of these three do you think was a neighbor to the man who fell into the hands of robbers?" The expert in the law replied, "The one who had mercy on him." Jesus told him, "Go and do likewise" (Luke 10:36–37 NIV).

The parable of the good Samaritan has worked its way into society's consciousness like no other parable Jesus told. The term "Good Samaritan" is used today to picture someone who takes time to help others. But the meaning of the parable goes much deeper than simply helping people in need—it's about reaching out in God's love and compassion even when it's inconvenient, unpopular, or costly.

 Connecting

Open your group with prayer. Thank God for all he has done in your group and among its members during the course of this study. Praise him for what he will do in your lives as you continue to walk with him.

1. Share one thing you learned or renewed in your life during this study of parables. Also, share with the group one thing you enjoyed about the study and the group.

2. Take time in this final session to connect with your spiritual partner. Turn to the *Personal Health Plan* and consider the "HOW are you surrendering your heart?" question. What has God been showing you through these sessions about his relationship to us and the world? Check in with each other about the progress you have made in your spiritual growth during this study. Talk about the possibility of continuing in your mentoring relationship outside your Bible study group.

 Growing

The parable of the good Samaritan is a model of how to love unconditionally. Jesus used the parable to show us that true love is demonstrated through action, regardless of race, object, or cost.

Read Luke 10:25–37 aloud.

3. The expert of verse 25 was probably an expert in the law of Moses and the traditions for applying it. (See the *Study Notes* for more about the law of Moses.) This lawyer stood up to ask his question as a show of respect. What clues indicate that his questions weren't honest efforts to learn wisdom from Jesus?

4. The lawyer quoted from Deuteronomy 6:5 and Leviticus 19:18, showing that he correctly understood that the law demanded devotion to God and love for others. Does it surprise you that Jesus and the lawyer agreed on what the core of Judaism was? Explain your thoughts.

5. Jesus says that to love your neighbor as yourself is a requirement for life. What does the lawyer's question in verse 29 indicate

about his understanding of Jesus's statement in verse 28? What should his response have been?

6. Jesus uses this parable to show that the lawyer is asking the wrong question. Read verses 30–35 and the *Study Notes* on Levites. What do you think Jesus means his hearers to think about the priest and the Levite in light of their actions?

How do you think the priest and Levite would answer the question, "Who is my neighbor?"

7. Samaritans were a despised ethnic group. For a similar impact in modern Christian America, Jesus might tell a story about two pastors (the priest and Levite) and a fundamentalist Muslim. Why do you think he chose such a person to be the hero of his story?

What are we meant to learn from this story?

8. How would you define love based on this story?

How does this compare to Jesus's demonstration of love on the cross? See Philippians 2:5–11 for help.

9. "Go and do likewise" is a command that applies to all people (v. 37). How can we do this?

Jesus is to all of us as the Samaritan was to the man in need. He gave his all for us. This parable asks us to do the same. Jesus wasn't thinking of himself when he left heaven's glory to come to earth, lived thirty years in humble service and humility, and went to the cross for our sins. He was thinking of us. That's what we are called to do.

 Developing

Jesus's parable of the good Samaritan demonstrates that loving your neighbor even means loving your enemies. In the parable Jesus answers the question, "Who is our neighbor?" The answer is: everyone—friends and enemies alike. How can we break the cycle of fear that keeps us from uncomfortable situations? Learn to trust the Lord!

10. What's next for your group? Will you continue to meet together? If so, the *Small Group Agreement* can help you talk through any changes you might want to make as you move forward. What will you study?

    As your group starts a new study, this is a great time to consider taking on a new role or change roles of service in your group. What new role will you take on for the next study? If you are uncertain, maybe your group members have some ideas for you. Remember you aren't making a lifetime commitment to the new role; it will only be for a few weeks. Also, consider sharing a role with another group member if you don't feel ready to serve solo.

Sharing

A true neighbor is willing to move beyond past pains and hurts to extend God's love to others. A true neighbor is willing to take a risk, as Jesus did for us on the cross.

11. Jesus also used stories, or parables, to demonstrate our need for salvation. Through these stories, he helped people see the error of their ways, leading them to turn to him. Your story can be just as powerful today. Turn to *Telling Your Story* in the *Appendix*. Review this with your spiritual partner. Begin developing your story by taking a few minutes to share briefly what your life was like before you knew Christ. (If you haven't yet committed your life to Christ or are not sure, you can find information about this in the *Sharing* section of *Session Three*. If you became a Christian at a very young age and don't remember what life was like before Christ, reflect on what you have seen in the life of someone close to you.) Make notes about this aspect of your story below and commit to writing

it out this week. Then, spend some time individually developing your complete story using the *Telling Your Story* exercise in the *Appendix*.

_____

_____

_____

12. If your group still needs to make decisions about continuing to meet after this session, have that discussion now. Talk about what you will study, who will lead, and where and when you will meet.

    Review your *Small Group Agreement* and evaluate how well you met your goals. Discuss any changes you want to make as you move forward. As your group starts a new study, this is a great time to take on a new role or change roles of service in your group. What new role will you take on? If you are uncertain, maybe your group members have some ideas for you. Remember you aren't making a lifetime commitment to the new role; it will only be for a few weeks. Maybe someone would like to share a role with you if you don't feel ready to serve solo.

 Surrendering

13. Close by praying for your prayer requests and take a couple of minutes to review the praises you have recorded on the *Prayer and Praise Report*. Thank God for what he's done in your group during this study.

Study Notes

Law of Moses (Mosaic Law and Law of the Lord): Usually refers to the first five books of the Old Testament, but sometimes to the entire Old Testament. At the foot of Mount Sinai, God showed his people the true function and beauty of his laws. The commandments were designed to lead Israel to a life of practical holiness. In them, people could see the nature of God and his plan for how they should live. The commands and guidelines were intended to direct the community to meet the needs of each individual in a loving and responsible manner. By Jesus's time, however, most people looked at the law the wrong way. They saw it as a means to prosperity in both this world and the next. And the scribes had built an elaborate system for interpreting and applying the law in order to assure God's protection from foreign invasion and natural disaster. Law keeping became an end in itself, not the means to fulfill God's ultimate law of love.

Levite: A descendant of the tribe of Levi. This name is generally used to refer to that portion of the tribe that was set apart for sanctuary service (1 Kings 8:4). A priest or a Levite might be expected to deliberately pass by a dying man, even a Jew, without helping him because contact with a dead body made a person unclean. An unclean person was unable to serve in the temple without undergoing inconvenient purification rituals. (See Lev. 21:1–6 for more information on the defilement of priests.) Also, the road from Jerusalem to Jericho was dangerous. Robbers hid along its steep, winding way, and many people would have been afraid to stop at what might have been an ambush. The priest and Levite were selfish, but not remarkably so, given the risk of stopping.

Reflections

Each day, read the daily verses and give prayerful consideration to what you learn about God, his Spirit, and his place in your life. Then record your thoughts, insights, or prayer in the Reflect section below the verses you read. On the sixth day record a summary of what you have learned over the entire week through this study.

Day 1. Jesus replied: "Love the Lord your God with all your heart and with all your soul and with all your mind." This is the first and greatest commandment. And the second is like it: "Love your neighbor as yourself." All the Law and the Prophets hang on these two commandments (Matt. 22:37–40 NIV).

REFLECT

_____

_____

_____

_____

Day 2. The commandments, "Do not commit adultery," "Do not murder," "Do not steal," "Do not covet," and whatever other commandment there may be, are summed up in this one rule: "Love your neighbor as yourself" (Rom. 13:9 NIV).

REFLECT

_____

_____

_____

_____

Day 3. "Which of these three do you think was a neighbor to the man who fell into the hands of robbers?" The expert in the law replied, "The one who had mercy on him." Jesus told him, "Go and do likewise" (Luke 10:36–37 NIV).

REFLECT

_____

_____

_____

_____

Day 4. The fear of man brings a snare, but he who trusts in the LORD will be exalted (Prov. 29:25 NASB).

REFLECT

_____

_____

_____

_____

Day 5. For God so loved the world that he gave his one and only Son, that whoever believes in him shall not perish but have eternal life (John 3:16 NIV).

REFLECT

_____

_____

_____

_____

Day 6. Use the following space to write any thoughts God has put in your heart and mind about the things we have looked at in this session and during your *Reflections* time this week.

SUMMARY

_____

_____

_____

_____

FREQUENTLY ASKED QUESTIONS

What do we do on the first night of our group?

Like all fun things in life—have a party! A "get to know you" coffee, dinner, or dessert is a great way to launch a new study. You may want to review the *Small Group Agreement* and share the names of a few friends you can invite to join you. But most importantly, have fun before your study time begins.

Where do we find new members for our group?

This can be challenging, especially for new groups that have only a few people or for existing groups that lose a few people along the way. We encourage you to pray with your group and then brainstorm a list of people from work, church, your neighborhood, your children's school, family, the gym, and so forth. Then have each group member invite several of the people on his or her list. Another good strategy is to ask church leaders to make an announcement that your group is open to new members.

No matter how you find members, it's vital that you stay on the lookout for new people to join your group. All groups tend to go through healthy attrition—the result of moves, releasing new leaders, ministry opportunities, and so forth—and if the group gets too small, it could be at risk of shutting down. If you and your group stay open, you'll be amazed at the people God sends your way. The next person just might become a friend for life. You never know!

How long will this group meet?

It's totally up to the group—once you come to the end of this study. Most groups meet weekly for at least their first six months together, but every other week can work as well. We strongly recommend that the group meet for the first six months on a weekly basis if at all possible. This allows for continuity, and if people miss a meeting they aren't gone for a whole month.

At the end of this study, each group member may decide whether he or she wants to continue on for another study. Some groups launch relationships that last for years, and others are stepping-stones into another group experience. Either way, enjoy the journey.

What if this group is not working for me?

Personality conflicts, life stage differences, geographical distance, level of spiritual maturity, or any number of things can cause you to feel the group doesn't work for you. Relax. Pray for God's direction, and at the end of this study decide whether to continue with this group or find another. You don't buy the first car you look at or marry the first person you date, and the same goes with a group. Don't bail out before the study is finished—God might have something to teach you. Also, don't run from conflict or prejudge people before you have given them a chance. God is still working in you too!

Who is the leader?

Most groups have an official leader. But ideally, the group will mature and members will share the facilitation of meetings. We have discovered that healthy groups share hosting and leading of the group. This model ensures that all members grow, give their unique contribution, and develop their gifts. This study guide and the Holy Spirit can keep things on track even when you share leadership. Christ has promised to be in your midst as you gather. Ultimately, God is your leader each step of the way.

How do we handle the child care needs in our group?

This can be a sensitive issue. We suggest that you empower the group to openly brainstorm solutions. You may try one option that works for a while and then adjust over time. Our favorite approach is for adults to meet in the living room or dining room, and share the cost of a babysitter (or two) who can be with the kids in a different part of the house. In this way, parents don't have to be away from their children all evening when their children are too young to be left at home. A second option is to use one home for the kids and a second home (close by) for the adults. A third idea is to rotate the responsibility of providing a lesson or care for the children either in the same home or in another home nearby. This can be an incredible blessing for kids. Finally, the most common idea is to decide that you need to have a night to invest in your spiritual lives individually or as a couple, and make your own arrangements for child care. No matter what decision the group makes, the best approach is to dialogue openly about both the problem and the solution.

SMALL GROUP AGREEMENT

Our Purpose

To transform our spiritual lives by cultivating our spiritual health in a healthy small group community. In addition, we:

_____

_____

_____

Our Values

Group Attendance	To give priority to the group meeting. We will call or e-mail if we will be late or absent. (Completing the *Small Group Calendar* will minimize this issue.)
Safe Environment	To help create a safe place where people can be heard and feel loved. (Please, no quick answers, snap judgments, or simple fixes.)
Respect Differences	To be gentle and gracious to people with different spiritual maturity, personal opinions, temperaments, or imperfections. We are all works in progress.
Confidentiality	To keep anything that is shared strictly confidential and within the group, and avoid sharing improper information about those outside the group.
Encouragement for Growth	To be not just takers but givers of life. We want to spiritually multiply our lives by serving others with our God-given gifts.

Welcome for Newcomers	To keep an open chair and share Jesus's dream of finding a shepherd for every sheep.
Shared Ownership	To remember that every member is a minister and to ensure that each attender will share a small team role or responsibility over time. (See the *Team Roles*.)
Rotating Hosts/ Leaders and Homes	To encourage different people to host the group in their homes, and to rotate the responsibility of facilitating each meeting. (See the *Small Group Calendar*.)

Our Expectations

- Refreshments/mealtimes _____
- Child care _____
- When we will meet (day of week) _____
- Where we will meet (place) _____
- We will begin at (time) _____ and end at _____
- We will do our best to have some or all of us attend a worship service together. Our primary worship service time will be _____
- Date of this agreement _____
- Date we will review this agreement again _____
- Who (other than the leader) will review this agreement at the end of this study _____

TEAM ROLES

The Bible makes clear that every member, not just the small group leader, is a minister in the body of Christ. In a healthy small group, every member takes on some small role or responsibility. It can be more fun and effective if you team up on these roles.

Review the team roles and responsibilities below, and have each member volunteer for a role or participate on a team. If someone doesn't know where to serve or is holding back, as a group, suggest a team or role. It's best to have one or two people on each team so you have each of the five purposes covered. Serving in even a small capacity will not only help your leader but also will make the group more fun for everyone. Don't hold back. Join a team!

The opportunities below are broken down by the five purposes and then by a *crawl* (beginning), *walk* (intermediate), or *run* (advanced) role. Try to cover at least the crawl and walk roles, and select a role that matches your group, your gifts, and your maturity.

Team Roles	Team Player(s)

CONNECTING TEAM (Fellowship and Community Building)

Crawl: Host a social event or group activity in the first week or two.

Walk: Create a list of uncommitted friends and then invite them to an open house or group social.

Run: Plan a twenty-four-hour retreat or weekend getaway for the group. Lead the *Connecting* time each week for the group.

GROWING TEAM (Discipleship and Spiritual Growth)

Crawl: Coordinate the spiritual partners for the group. Facilitate a three- or four-person discussion circle during the Bible study portion of your meeting. Coordinate the discussion circles.

Walk: Tabulate the *Personal Health Plans* in a summary to let people know how you're doing as a group. Encourage personal devotions through group discussions and pairing up with spiritual (accountability) partners.

Run: Take the group on a prayer walk, or plan a day of solitude, fasting, or personal retreat.

SERVING TEAM (Discovering Your God-Given Design for Ministry)

Crawl: Ensure that every member finds a group role or team he or she enjoys.

Walk: Have every member take a gift test and determine your group's gifts. Plan a ministry project together.

Run: Help each member decide on a way to use his or her unique gifts somewhere in the church.

SHARING TEAM (Sharing and Evangelism)

Crawl: Coordinate the group's *Prayer and Praise Report* of friends and family who don't know Christ.

Walk: Search for group mission opportunities and plan a cross-cultural group activity.

Run: Take a small group "vacation" to host a six-week group in your neighborhood or office. Then come back together with your current group.

SURRENDERING TEAM (Surrendering Your Heart to Worship)

Crawl: Maintain the group's *Prayer and Praise Report* or journal.

Walk: Lead a brief time of worship each week (at the beginning or end of your meeting).

Run: Plan a more unique time of worship.

53

SMALL GROUP CALENDAR

Planning and calendaring can help ensure the greatest participation at every meeting. At the end of each meeting, review this calendar. Be sure to include a regular rotation of host homes and leaders, and don't forget birthdays, socials, church events, holidays, and mission/ministry projects.

Date	Lesson	Dessert/Meal	Role

PERSONAL HEALTH ASSESSMENT

	Just Beginning	Getting Going	Well Developed

CONNECTING with God's Family

I am deepening my understanding of and friendship with God in community with others.   1 2 3 4 5

I am growing in my ability both to share and to show my love to others.   1 2 3 4 5

I am willing to share my real needs for prayer and support from others.   1 2 3 4 5

I am resolving conflict constructively and am willing to forgive others.   1 2 3 4 5

CONNECTING Total   ____

GROWING to Be Like Christ

I have a growing relationship with God through regular time in the Bible and in prayer (spiritual habits).   1 2 3 4 5

I am experiencing more of the characteristics of Jesus Christ (love, patience, gentleness, courage, self-control, etc.) in my life.   1 2 3 4 5

I am avoiding addictive behaviors (food, television, busyness, and the like) to meet my needs.   1 2 3 4 5

I am spending time with a Christian friend (spiritual partner) who celebrates and challenges my spiritual growth.   1 2 3 4 5

GROWING Total   ____

55

	Just Beginning	Getting Going	Well Developed

DEVELOPING Your Gifts to Serve Others

I have discovered and am further developing my unique God-given design. 1 2 3 4 5

I am regularly praying for God to show me opportunities to serve him and others. 1 2 3 4 5

I am serving in a regular (once a month or more) ministry in the church or community. 1 2 3 4 5

I am a team player in my small group by sharing some group role or responsibility. 1 2 3 4 5

DEVELOPING Total _____

SHARING Your Life Mission Every Day

I am cultivating relationships with non-Christians and praying for God to give me natural opportunities to share his love. 1 2 3 4 5

I am praying and learning about where God can use me and our group cross-culturally for missions. 1 2 3 4 5

I am investing my time in another person or group who needs to know Christ. 1 2 3 4 5

I am regularly inviting unchurched or unconnected friends to my church or small group. 1 2 3 4 5

SHARING Total _____

SURRENDERING Your Life for God's Pleasure

I am experiencing more of the presence and power of God in my everyday life. 1 2 3 4 5

I am faithfully attending services and my small group to worship God. 1 2 3 4 5

I am seeking to please God by surrendering every area of my life (health, decisions, finances, relationships, future, etc.) to him. 1 2 3 4 5

I am accepting the things I cannot change and becoming increasingly grateful for the life I've been given. 1 2 3 4 5

SURRENDERING Total _____

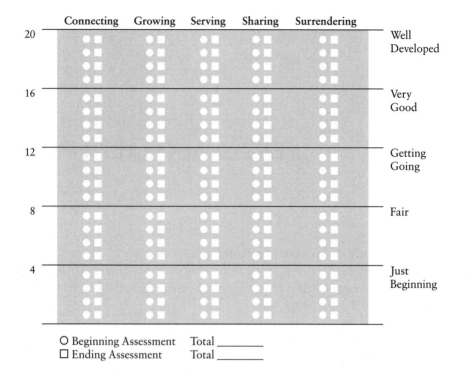

O Beginning Assessment   Total _____
☐ Ending Assessment   Total _____

PERSONAL HEALTH PLAN

This worksheet could become your single most important feature in this study. On it you can record your personal priorities before the Father. It will help you live a healthy spiritual life, balancing all five of God's purposes.

PURPOSE	PLAN
CONNECT	WHO are you connecting with spiritually?
GROW	WHAT is your next step for growth?
DEVELOP	WHERE are you serving?
SHARE	WHEN are you shepherding another in Christ?
SURRENDER	HOW are you surrendering your heart to God?

DATE	MY PROGRESS	PARTNER'S PROGRESS

Personal Health Plan

DATE	MY PROGRESS	PARTNER'S PROGRESS

SAMPLE PERSONAL HEALTH PLAN

This worksheet could become your single most important feature in this study. On it you can record your personal priorities before the Father. It will help you live a healthy spiritual life, balancing all five of God's purposes.

PURPOSE	PLAN
CONNECT	WHO are you connecting with spiritually?
	Bill and I will meet weekly by e-mail or phone
GROW	WHAT is your next step for growth?
	Regular devotions or journaling my prayers 2×/week
DEVELOP	WHERE are you serving?
	Serving in children's ministry Go through GIFTS Assessment
SHARE	WHEN are you shepherding another in Christ?
	Shepherding Bill at lunch or hosting a starter group in the fall
SURRENDER	HOW are you surrendering your heart?
	Help with our teenager New job situation

DATE	MY PROGRESS	PARTNER'S PROGRESS
3/5	Talked during our group	Figured out our goals together
3/12	Missed our time together	Missed our time together
3/26	Met for coffee and review of my goals	Met for coffee
4/10	E-mailed prayer requests	Bill sent me his prayer requests
5/5	Great start on personal journaling	Read Mark 1–6 in one sitting!
5/12	Traveled and not doing well this week	Journaled about Christ as healer
5/26	Back on track	Busy and distracted; asked for prayer
6/1	Need to call Children's Pastor	
6/26	Group did a serving project together	Agreed to lead group worship
6/30	Regularly rotating leadership	Led group worship–great job!
7/5	Called Jim to see if he's open to joining our group	Wanted to invite somebody, but didn't
7/12	Preparing to start a group in fall	
7/30	Group prayed for me	Told friend something I'm learning about Christ
8/5	Overwhelmed but encouraged	Scared to lead worship
8/15	Felt heard and more settled	Issue with wife
8/30	Read book on teens	Glad he took on his fear

SPIRITUAL GIFTS INVENTORY

A spiritual gift is given to each of us as a means of helping the entire church.

1 Corinthians 12:7 (NLT)

A spiritual gift is a special ability, given by the Holy Spirit to every believer at their conversion. Although spiritual gifts are given when the Holy Spirit enters new believers, their use and purpose need to be understood and developed as we grow spiritually. A spiritual gift is much like a muscle; the more you use it, the stronger it becomes.

A Few Truths about Spiritual Gifts

1. Only believers have spiritual gifts. 1 Corinthians 2:14
2. You can't earn or work for a spiritual gift. Ephesians 4:7
3. The Holy Spirit decides what gifts I get. 1 Corinthians 12:11
4. I am to develop the gifts God gives me. Romans 11:29; 2 Timothy 1:6
5. It's a sin to waste the gifts God gave me. 1 Corinthians 4:1–2; Matthew 25:14–30
6. Using my gifts honors God and expands me. John 15:8

Gifts Inventory

God wants us to know what spiritual gift(s) he has given us. One person can have many gifts. The goal is to find the areas in which the Holy Spirit seems to have supernaturally empowered our service to others. These gifts are to be used to minister to others and build up the body of Christ.

There are four main lists of gifts found in the Bible in Romans 12:3–8; 1 Corinthians 12:1–11, 27–31; Ephesians 4:11–12; and 1 Peter 4:9–11. There are other passages that mention or illustrate gifts not included in these lists. As you read through this list, prayerfully consider whether the biblical definition describes you. Remember, you can have more than one gift, but everyone has at least one.

ADMINISTRATION (Organization)—1 Corinthians 12
This is the ability to recognize the gifts of others and recruit them to a ministry. It is the ability to organize and manage people, resources, and time for effective ministry.

APOSTLE—1 Corinthians 12
This is the ability to start new churches/ventures and oversee their development.

DISCERNMENT—1 Corinthians 12
This is the ability to distinguish between the spirit of truth and the spirit of error; to detect inconsistencies in another's life and confront in love.

ENCOURAGEMENT (Exhortation)—Romans 12
This is the ability to motivate God's people to apply and act on biblical principles, especially when they are discouraged or wavering in their faith. It is also the ability to bring out the best in others and challenge them to develop their potential.

EVANGELISM—Ephesians 4
This is the ability to communicate the gospel of Jesus Christ to unbelievers in a positive, nonthreatening way and to sense opportunities to share Christ and lead people to respond with faith.

FAITH—1 Corinthians 12

This is the ability to trust God for what cannot be seen and to act on God's promise, regardless of what the circumstances indicate. This includes a willingness to risk failure in pursuit of a God-given vision, expecting God to handle the obstacles.

GIVING—Romans 12

This is the ability to generously contribute material resources and/or money beyond the 10 percent tithe so that the church may grow and be strengthened. It includes the ability to manage money so it may be given to support the ministry of others.

HOSPITALITY—1 Peter 4:9–10

This is the ability to make others, especially strangers, feel warmly welcomed, accepted, and comfortable in the church family and the ability to coordinate factors that promote fellowship.

LEADERSHIP—Romans 12

This is the ability to clarify and communicate the purpose and direction ("vision") of a ministry in a way that attracts others to get involved, including the ability to motivate others, by example, to work together in accomplishing a ministry goal.

MERCY—Romans 12

This is the ability to manifest practical, compassionate, cheerful love toward suffering members of the body of Christ.

PASTORING (Shepherding)—Ephesians 4

This is the ability to care for the spiritual needs of a group of believers and equip them for ministry. It is also the ability to nurture a small group in spiritual growth and assume responsibility for their welfare.

PREACHING—Romans 12

This is the ability to publicly communicate God's Word in an inspired way that convinces unbelievers and both challenges and comforts believers.

SERVICE—Romans 12

This is the ability to recognize unmet needs in the church family, and take the initiative to provide practical assistance quickly, cheerfully, and without a need for recognition.

TEACHING—Ephesians 4

This is the ability to educate God's people by clearly explaining and applying the Bible in a way that causes them to learn; it is the ability to equip and train other believers for ministry.

WISDOM—1 Corinthians 12

This is the ability to understand God's perspective on life situations and share those insights in a simple, understandable way.

TELLING YOUR STORY

First, don't underestimate the power of your testimony. Revelation 12:11 says, "They have defeated [Satan] by the blood of the Lamb and by their testimony. And they did not love their lives so much that they were afraid to die" (NLT).

A simple three-point approach is very effective in communicating your personal testimony. The approach focuses on before you trusted Christ, how you surrendered to him, and the difference in you since you've been walking with him. If you became a Christian at a very young age and don't remember what life was like before Christ, reflect on what you have seen in the lives of others. Before you begin, pray and ask God to give you the right words.

Before You Knew Christ

Simply tell what your life was like before you surrendered to Christ. What was the key problem, emotion, situation, or attitude you were dealing with? What motivated you? What were your actions? How did you try to satisfy your inner needs? Create an interesting picture of your preconversion life and problems, and then explain what created a need and interest in Christian things.

How You Came to Know Christ

How were you converted? Simply tell the events and circumstances that caused you to consider Christ as the solution to your needs. Take time to identify the steps that brought you to the point of trusting Christ. Where were you? What was happening at the time? What people or problems influenced your decision?

The Difference Christ Has Made in Your Life

What is different about your life in Christ? How has his forgiveness impacted you? How have your thoughts, attitudes, and emotions changed? What problems have been resolved or changed? Share how Christ is meeting your needs and what a relationship with him means to you now. This should be the largest part of your story.

Tips

- Don't use jargon: don't sound churchy, preachy, or pious.
- Stick to the point. Your conversion and new life in Christ should be the main points.
- Be specific. Include events, genuine feelings, and personal insights, both before and after conversion, which people would be interested in and that clarify your main point. This makes your testimony easier to relate to. Assume you are sharing with someone with no knowledge of the Christian faith.
- Be current. Tell what is happening in your life with God now, today.
- Be honest. Don't exaggerate or portray yourself as living a perfect life with no problems. This is not realistic. The simple truth of what God has done in your life is all the Holy Spirit needs to convict someone of their sin and convince them of his love and grace.
- Remember, it's the Holy Spirit who convicts. You need only be obedient and tell your story.
- When people reply to your efforts to share with statements like "I don't believe in God," "I don't believe the Bible is God's Word," or "How can a loving God allow suffering?" how can we respond to these replies?

- Above all, keep a positive attitude. Don't be defensive.
- Be sincere. This will speak volumes about your confidence in your faith.
- Don't be offended. It's not you they are rejecting.
- Pray—silently on-the-spot. Don't proceed without asking for God's help about the specific question. Seek his guidance on how, or if, you should proceed at this time.
- In God's wisdom, choose to do one of the following:
  - Postpone sharing at this time.
  - Answer their objections, if you can.
  - Promise to research their questions and return answers later.

Step 1. Everywhere Jesus went he used stories, or parables, to demonstrate our need for salvation. Through these stories, he helped people see the error of their ways, leading them to turn to him. Your story can be just as powerful today. Begin to develop your story by sharing what your life was like before you knew Christ. (If you haven't yet committed your life to Christ, or became a Christian at a very young age and don't remember what life was like before Christ, reflect on what you have seen in the life of someone close to you.) Make notes about this aspect of your story below and commit to writing it out this week.

_____

_____

_____

Step 2. Sit in groups of two or three people for this discussion. Review the "How You Came to Know Christ" section. Begin to develop this part of your story by sharing within your circle. Make notes about this aspect of your story below and commit to writing it out this week.

_____

_____

_____

Step 2b. Connecting: Go around the group and share about a time you were stopped cold while sharing Christ, by a question you couldn't answer. What happened?

Step 2c. Sharing: Previously we talked about the questions and objections we receive that stop us from continuing to share our faith with someone. These questions/objections might include:

- "I don't believe in God."
- "I don't believe the Bible is God's Word."
- "How can a loving God allow suffering?"

How can we respond to these replies?

Step 3. Subgroup into groups of two or three people for this discussion. Review "The Difference Christ Has Made in Your Life" section. Share the highlights of this part of your story within your circle. Make notes about this aspect of your story below and commit to writing it out this week.

Step 3b. Story: There's nothing more exciting than a brand-new believer. My wife became a Christian four years before I met her. She was a flight attendant at the time. Her zeal to introduce others to Jesus was reminiscent of the woman at the well who ran and got the whole town out to see Jesus.

My wife immediately began an international organization of Christian flight attendants for fellowship and for reaching out to others in their profession. She organized events where many people came to Christ, and bid for trips with another flight attendant who was a Christian so they could witness on the planes. They even bid for the shorter trips so they could talk to as many different people as possible. They had a goal for every flight to talk to at least one person about Christ, and to be encouraged by at least one person who already knew him. God met that request every time.

In her zeal, however, she went home to her family over the holidays and vacations and had little or no success. Later she would realize that she pressed them too hard. Jesus said a prophet is without honor in his own town, and I think the same goes for family. That's because members of your family think they know you, and are more likely to ignore changes, choosing instead to see you as they've always seen you. "Isn't this the carpenter's son—the son of Joseph?" they said of Jesus. "Don't we know this guy?"

With family members you have to walk with Christ openly and be patient. Change takes time. And remember, we don't save anyone. We just introduce them to Jesus through telling our own story. God does the rest.

Step 4. As a group, review *Telling Your Story*. Share which part of your story is the most difficult for you to tell. Which is the easiest for you? If you have time, a few of you share your story with the group.

Step 5. Throughout this study we have had the opportunity to develop our individual testimonies. One way your group can serve each other is to provide a safe forum for "practicing" telling your stories. Continue to take turns sharing your testimonies now. Set a time limit—say two to three minutes each. Don't miss this great opportunity to get to know one another better and encourage each other's growth too.

SERVING COMMUNION

Churches vary in their treatment of communion (or the Lord's Supper). We offer one simple form by which a small group can share this experience together. You can adapt this as necessary, or omit it from your group altogether, depending on your church's beliefs.

Steps in Serving Communion

1. Open by sharing about God's love, forgiveness, grace, mercy, commitment, tenderheartedness, faithfulness, etc., out of your personal journey (connect with the stories of those in the room).
2. Read one or several of the passages listed below.
3. Pray and pass the bread around the circle.
4. When everyone has been served, remind them that this represents Jesus's broken body on their behalf. Simply state, "Jesus said, 'Do this in remembrance of me' (Luke 22:19 NIV). Let us eat together," and eat the bread as a group.
5. Then read the rest of the passage: "In the same way, after the supper he took the cup, saying, 'This cup is the new covenant in my blood, which is poured out for you'" (Luke 22:20 NIV).
6. Pray, and serve the cups, either by passing a small tray, serving them individually, or having members pick up a cup from the table.
7. When everyone has been served, remind them the juice represents Christ's blood shed for them, then simply state, "Take and drink in remembrance of him. Let us drink together."
8. Finish by singing a simple song, listening to a praise song, or having a time of prayer in thanks to God.

Communion passages: Matthew 26:26–29; Mark 14:22–25; Luke 22:14–20; 1 Corinthians 10:16–21; 11:17–34.

PERFORMING A FOOTWASHING

Scripture: John 13:1–17. Jesus makes it quite clear to his disciples that his position as the Father's Son includes being a servant rather than power and glory only. To properly understand the scene and the intention of Jesus, we must realize that the washing of feet was the duty of slaves and indeed of non-Jewish rather than Jewish slaves. Jesus placed himself in the position of a servant. He displayed to the disciples self-sacrifice and love. In view of his majesty, only the symbolic position of a slave was adequate to open their eyes and keep them from lofty illusions. The point of footwashing, then, is to correct the attitude that Jesus discerned in the disciples. It constitutes the permanent basis for mutual service, service in your group and for the community around you, which is the responsibility of all Christians.

When to Implement

There are three primary places we would recommend you insert a footwashing: during a break in the Surrendering section of your group; during a break in the Growing section of your group; or at the closing of your group. A special time of prayer for each person as he or she gets his or her feet washed can be added to the footwashing time.

SURRENDERING AT THE CROSS

Surrendering everything to God is one of the most challenging aspects of following Jesus. It involves a relationship built on trust and faith. Each of us is in a different place on our spiritual journey. Some of us have known the Lord for many years, some are new in our faith, and some may still be checking God out. Regardless, we all have things that we still want control over—things we don't want to give to God because we don't know what he will do with them. These things are truly more important to us than God is—they have become our god.

We need to understand that God wants us to be completely devoted to him. If we truly love God with all our heart, soul, strength, and mind (Luke 10:27), we will be willing to give him everything.

Steps in Surrendering at the Cross

1. You will need some small pieces of paper and pens or pencils for people to write down the things they want to sacrifice/surrender to God.
2. If you have a wooden cross, hammers, and nails you can have the members nail their sacrifices to the cross. If you don't have a wooden cross, get creative. Think of another way to symbolically relinquish the sacrifices to God. You might use a fireplace to burn them in the fire as an offering to the Lord. The point is giving to the Lord whatever hinders your relationship with him.

3. Create an atmosphere conducive to quiet reflection and prayer. Whatever this quiet atmosphere looks like for your group, do the best you can to create a peaceful time to meet with God.

4. Once you are settled, prayerfully think about the points below. Let the words and thoughts draw you into a heart-to-heart connection with your Lord Jesus Christ.

   ☐ *Worship him.* Ask God to change your viewpoint so you can worship him through a surrendered spirit.

   ☐ *Humble yourself.* Surrender doesn't happen without humility. James 4:6–7 says: "'God opposes the proud but gives grace to the humble.' Submit yourselves, then, to God" (NIV).

   ☐ *Surrender your mind, will, and emotions.* This is often the toughest part of surrendering. What do you sense God urging you to give him so you can have the kind of intimacy he desires with you? Our hearts yearn for this kind of connection with him; let go of the things that stand between you.

   ☐ *Write out your prayer.* Write out your prayer of sacrifice and surrender to the Lord. This may be an attitude, a fear, a person, a job, a possession—anything that God reveals is a hindrance to your relationship with him.

5. After writing out your sacrifice, take it to the cross and offer it to the Lord. Nail your sacrifice to the cross, or burn it as a sacrifice in the fire.

6. Close by singing, praying together, or taking communion. Make this time as short or as long as seems appropriate for your group.

Surrendering to God is life-changing and liberating. God desires that we be overcomers! First John 4:4 says, "You, dear children, are from God and have overcome . . . because the one who is in you is greater than the one who is in the world" (NIV).

JOURNALING 101

Henri Nouwen says effective and lasting ministry *for* God grows out of a quiet place alone *with* God. This is why journaling is so important.

The greatest adventure of our lives is found in the daily pursuit of knowing, growing in, serving, sharing, and worshiping Christ forever. This is the essence of a purposeful life: to see all these biblical purposes fully formed and balanced in our lives. Only then are we "complete in Christ" (Col. 1:28 NASB).

David poured his heart out to God by writing psalms. The book of Psalms contains many of his honest conversations with God in written form, including expressions of every imaginable emotion on every aspect of his life. Like David, we encourage you to select a strategy to integrate God's Word and journaling into your devotional time. Use any of the following resources:

- Bible
- Bible reading plan
- Devotional
- Topical Bible study plan

Before and after you read a portion of God's Word, speak to God in honest reflection in the form of a written prayer. You may begin this time by simply finishing the sentence "Father, . . . ," "Yesterday, Lord, . . . ," or "Thank you, God, for, ..." Share with him where you are at the present moment; express your hurts, disappointments, frustrations, blessings, victories, and gratefulness. Whatever you do with your journal, make a plan that fits you, so you'll have a positive experience. Consider sharing highlights of your progress and experiences with some or all of your group members, especially your spiritual partner. You may find they want to join and even encourage you in this journey. Most of all, enjoy the ride and cultivate a more authentic, growing walk with God.

PRAYER AND PRAISE REPORT

Briefly share your prayer requests with the large group, making notations below. Then gather in small groups of two to four to pray for each other.

Date: _____

Prayer Requests

_____

_____

_____

_____

_____

Praise Reports

_____

_____

_____

_____

_____

Prayer and Praise Report

Briefly share your prayer requests with the large group, making notations below. Then gather in small groups of two to four to pray for each other.

Date: _____

Prayer Requests

_____

_____

_____

_____

_____

Praise Reports

_____

_____

_____

_____

_____

Prayer and Praise Report

Briefly share your prayer requests with the large group, making notations below. Then gather in small groups of two to four to pray for each other.

Date: _____

Prayer Requests

_____

_____

_____

_____

_____

Praise Reports

_____

_____

_____

_____

_____

Prayer and Praise Report

Briefly share your prayer requests with the large group, making notations below. Then gather in small groups of two to four to pray for each other.

Date: _____

Prayer Requests

_____

_____

_____

_____

_____

Praise Reports

_____

_____

_____

_____

_____

SMALL GROUP ROSTER

Name	Address	Phone	E-mail Address	Team or Role	When/How to Contact You
Bill Jones	7 Alvalar Street L.F. 92665	766-2255	bjones@aol.com	Socials	Evenings After 5

(Pass your book around your group at your first meeting to get every-one's name and contact information.)

Name	Address	Phone	E-mail Address	Team or Role	When/How to Contact You

LEADING FOR THE FIRST TIME
LEADERSHIP 101

Sweaty palms are a healthy sign. The Bible says God is gracious to the humble. Remember who is in control; the time to worry is when you're not worried. Those who are soft in heart (and sweaty-palmed) are those whom God is sure to speak through.

Seek support. Ask your leader, coleader, or close friend to pray for you and prepare with you before the session. Walking through the study will help you anticipate potentially difficult questions and discussion topics.

Bring your uniqueness to the study. Lean into who you are and how God wants you to uniquely lead the study.

Prepare. Prepare. Prepare. Go through the session several times. If you are using the DVD, listen to the teaching segment and *Leader Lifter*. Consider writing in a journal or fasting for a day to prepare yourself for what God wants to do.

Don't wait until the last minute to prepare.

Ask for feedback so you can grow. Perhaps in an e-mail or on cards handed out at the study, have everyone write down three things you did well and one thing you could improve on. Don't get defensive, but show an openness to learn and grow.

Prayerfully consider launching a new group. This doesn't need to happen overnight, but God's heart is for this to happen over time. Not all Christians are called to be leaders or teachers, but we are all called to be "shepherds" of a few someday.

Share with your group what God is doing in your heart. God is searching for those whose hearts are fully his. Share your trials and victories. We promise that people will relate.

Prayerfully consider whom you would like to pass the baton to next week. It's only fair. God is ready for the next member of your group to go on the faith journey you just traveled. Make it fun, and expect God to do the rest.

LEADER'S NOTES
INTRODUCTION

Congratulations! You have responded to the call to help shepherd Jesus's flock. There are few other tasks in the family of God that surpass the contribution you will be making. We have provided you several ways to prepare for this role. Between the *Read Me First*, these *Leader's Notes*, and the *Watch This First* and *Leader Lifter* segments on the optional *Deepening Life Together: Parables* Video Teaching DVD, you'll have all you need to do a great job of leading your group. Just don't forget, you are not alone. God knew that you would be asked to lead this group and he won't let you down. In Hebrews 13:5b God promises us, "Never will I leave you; never will I forsake you" (NIV).

Your role as leader is to create a safe, warm environment for your group. As a leader, your most important job is to create an atmosphere where people are willing to talk honestly about what the topics discussed in this study have to do with them. Be available before people arrive so you can greet them at the door. People are naturally nervous at a new group, so a hug or handshake can help put them at ease. Before you start leading your group, a little preparation will give you confidence. Review the *Read Me First* at the front of your study guide so you'll understand the purpose of each section, enabling you to help your group understand it as well.

If you're new to leading a group, congratulations and thank you; this will be a life-changing experience for you also. We have provided these *Leader's Notes* to help new leaders begin well.

It's important in your first meeting to make sure group members understand that things shared personally and in prayer must remain confidential. Also, be careful not to dominate the group discussion,

84

but facilitate it and encourage others to join in and share. And lastly, have fun.

Take a moment at the beginning of your first meeting to orient the group to one principle that undergirds this study: A healthy small group balances the purposes of the church. Most small groups emphasize Bible study, fellowship, and prayer. But God has called us to reach out to others as well. He wants us to do what Jesus teaches, not just learn about it.

Preparing for each meeting ahead of time. Take the time to review the session, the *Leader's Notes*, and *Leader Lifter* for the session before each session. Also write down your answers to each question. Pay special attention to exercises that ask group members to *do* something. These exercises will help your group live out what the Bible teaches, not just talk about it. Be sure you understand how the exercises work, and bring any supplies you might need, such as paper or pens. Pray for your group members by name at least once between sessions and before each session. Use the *Prayer and Praise Report* so you will remember their prayer requests. Ask God to use your time together to touch the heart of every person. Expect God to give you the opportunity to talk with those he wants you to encourage or challenge in a special way.

Don't try to go it alone. Pray for God to help you. Ask other members of your group to help by taking on some small role. In the *Appendix* you'll find the *Team Roles* pages with some suggestions to get people involved. Leading is more rewarding if you give group members opportunities to help. Besides, helping group members discover their individual gifts for serving or even leading the group will bless all of you.

Consider asking a few people to come early to help set up, pray, and introduce newcomers to others. Even if everyone is new, they don't know that yet and may be shy when they arrive. You might give people roles like setting up name tags or handing out drinks. This could be a great way to spot a co-leader.

Subgrouping. If your group has more than seven people, break into discussion groups of three to four people for the *Growing* and *Surrendering* sections each week. People will connect more with the study and each other when they have more opportunity to participate. Smaller discussion circles encourage quieter people to talk more and tend to minimize the effects of more vocal or dominant members. Also, people who are unaccustomed to praying aloud will feel more comfortable praying within a smaller group of people. Share prayer requests in the larger group and then break into smaller groups to pray for each other. People are more willing to pray in small circles if they know that the whole group will hear all the prayer requests.

Memorizing Scripture. At the start of each session you will find a memory verse—a verse for the group to memorize each week. Encourage your group members to do this. Memorizing God's Word is both directed and celebrated throughout the Bible, either explicitly ("Your word I have hidden in my heart, that I might not sin against You" [Ps. 119:11 NKJV]), or implicitly, as in the example of our Lord ("He departed to the mountain to pray" [Mark 6:46 NKJV]).

Anyone who has memorized Scripture can confirm the amazing spiritual benefits that result from this practice. Don't miss out on the opportunity to encourage your group to grow in the knowledge of God's Word through Scripture memorization.

Reflections. We've provided opportunity for a personal time with God using the *Reflections* at the end of each session. Don't press seekers to do this, but just remind the group that every believer should have a plan for personal time with God.

Inviting new people. Cast the vision, as Jesus did, to be inclusive not exclusive. Ask everyone to prayerfully think of people who would enjoy or benefit from a group like this—then invite them. The beginning of a new study is a great time to welcome a few people into your circle. Don't worry about ending up with too many people—you can always have one discussion circle in the living room and another in the dining room.

For Deeper Study (Optional). We have included a *For Deeper Study* section in each session. *For Deeper Study* provides additional passages for individual study on the topic of each session. If your group likes to do deeper Bible study, consider having members study the *For Deeper Study* passages for homework. Then, during the *Growing* portion of your meeting, you can share the high points of what you've learned.

LEADER'S NOTES
SESSIONS

Session One The Parable of the Prodigal Son

Connecting

1. We've designed this study for both new and established groups, and for both seekers and the spiritually mature. New groups will need to invest more time building relationships with each other. Established groups often want to dig deeper into Bible study and application. Regardless of whether your group is new or has been together for a while, be sure to take time to connect at this first session.

2. Each session will include an icebreaker question that should help to set the tone for the *Growing* section of your group time. It's important in this first session to allow time for everyone to participate in this icebreaker.

3. A very important item in this first session is the *Small Group Agreement*. An agreement helps clarify your group's priorities and cast new vision for what the group can become. You can find this in the *Appendix* of this study guide. We've found that groups that talk about these values up front and commit to an agreement benefit significantly. They work through conflicts long before people get to the point of frustration, so there's a lot less pain.

   Take some time to review this agreement before your meeting. Then during your meeting, read the agreement aloud to the entire group. If some people have concerns about a specific item or the agreement as a whole, be sensitive to their concerns. Explain that tens of thousands of groups use agreements like this one as a simple tool for building trust and group health over time.

   As part of this discussion, we recommend talking about shared ownership of the group. It's important that each member have a role. See the

Appendix to learn more about *Team Roles*. This is a great tool to get this important practice launched in your group.

Also, you will find a *Small Group Calendar* in the *Appendix* for use in planning your group meetings and roles. Take a look at the calendar prior to your first meeting and point it out to the group so that each person can note when and where the group will meet, who will bring snacks, any important upcoming events (birthdays, anniversaries), etc.

Growing

Have someone read Bible passages aloud. It's a good idea to ask ahead of time, because not everyone is comfortable reading aloud in public.

4. The son's actions give a picture of all sinners. After refusing any relationship with his father by defying his word and customs, the son chooses a life of sinful self-indulgence—prodigal living (v. 12). Requesting his inheritance while his father was still alive was like wishing his father was dead. Possibly, a nagging need for independence or need to be free of responsibility drove him. We can assume that the son planned his departure—it was not a spur-of-the-moment thing—as he took everything and left within a few days (v. 13).

5. God has given us free will to make our own choices. For this reason, the father agreed to his son's request, even though it likely hurt him greatly.

6. Encourage the group to talk about how relationship problems, stress of busyness, work, responsibilities, etc., often precipitate a desire to flee. When we try to run our lives on our own power, we become stressed and disoriented, causing the desire to flee. When we think only of ourselves and act accordingly, we are acting selfishly.

7. The son's sin separated him from his father; likewise, sin separates us from God.

8. The son's wasteful extravagance and a famine in the land left him destitute—feeding swine in some pagan village to survive (v. 15). But it was not enough to sustain him and no one helped him. He would have eaten the pigs' food if he could (v. 16). Jews would never allow themselves to come into contact with pigs, so Deuteronomy 14:8 shows us how far from righteousness the son had fallen. Nothing could be more degrading to a Jew.

9. The prodigal finally came to his senses and decided to go home and accept whatever was there for him (vv. 17–19); he planned to repent of his selfishness and tell his father he was sorry. The son would have known that his father no longer had anything to give him because when the inheritance was given, it was to both sons. The father would be living on earnings from the inheritance, but the inheritance now belonged to the sons. He expected nothing (for he had left no personal possessions behind) and hoped to be

allowed to be called a slave. This is a sign of true repentance—he turned from his evil ways with no expectation for what would happen to him.

10. The father had been watching and waiting for his son to return (v. 20). When he saw him, he ran to greet him. He was eager and joyous at the return of his son. His eagerness to forgive was so great that the son didn't even get to finish his apology (v. 21). Our Father in heaven watches and waits for the return of his children as well.

11. The father gave his son honor (the best robe), authority (a ring), acceptance (sandals for his feet: sandals were not usually worn by slaves), and a celebration of the event of his return (fine feast symbolizing salvation's blessings). See Genesis 41:42 and Zechariah 3:4 for additional insight on verse 22. The father poured out his love and expressed his joy that his once lost son had now been found—symbolizing the divine mercy of God. Just as the angels in heaven celebrate when a person repents and turns to the Lord, the father celebrated the return of his son. See Ephesians 2:5 and Colossians 2:13 for additional insight on verse 24.

12. It is not easy for the older brother to embrace the return of his brother. He does not have the love of the father. This parallels the feeling of the Pharisees toward Jesus and his disciples. The elder son symbolizes the Pharisees and other religious leaders, who had access to God's truth but no sense of sin, no real love for the Father, and no interest in repentant sinners. They didn't share God's joy.

13. Speaking to a parent in this way (v. 29) was contemptuous. It seems unlikely that he was the obedient son he claimed to be. And he did not recognize his own sin. Even his actions of the moment were a transgression of his father's wishes. The older son's reaction parallels the Pharisees' complaining about Jesus in verse 2: But the Pharisees and the teachers of the law muttered, "This man welcomes sinners and eats with them." He held only contempt for his brother and was begrudging even the love that the father showed to the prodigal son. The son's words also reveal that he thought his relationship with his father was based on his work. He was obedient (to a point) because of the expected reward, not out of love for his father.

14. The inheritance has already been distributed (v. 12). The older son already has everything the father has to give him—money and possessions—and he also has his love. People like the older brother have trouble believing that God's vast love and riches are already theirs. In a way, the older brother is the true runaway in this story, for he has never truly come home to trust his father.

15. God will always be waiting for his children to return to him, and there will always be those who refuse to join the party. Jesus is telling the Pharisees and all who refuse to go to the celebration feast that this is a refusal to enter the kingdom that Jesus offers to everyone. As leader, you should make it okay

for people to admit to having traits of either the older or younger brother. Some group members may relate to both.

Sharing

Jesus wants all of his disciples to help outsiders connect with him, to know him personally. This section should provide an opportunity to go beyond Bible study to biblical living.

17. We provided a *Circles of Life* diagram for you and the group to use to help you identify people who need to be connected in Christian community. When people are asked why they never go to church, they often say, "No one ever invited me." Remind the group that our responsibility is to invite people, but we are not responsible for how they respond. Talk to the group about the importance of inviting people; remind them that healthy small groups make a habit of inviting friends, neighbors, unconnected church members, co-workers, etc., to join their groups or join them at a weekend service. When people get connected to a group of new friends, they often join the church.

    The *Circles of Life* represent one of the values of the *Small Group Agreement* "Welcome for Newcomers." Some groups fear that newcomers will interrupt the intimacy that members have built over time. However, groups generally gain strength with the infusion of new blood. It's like a river of living water flowing into a stagnant pond. Some groups remain permanently open, while others open periodically, such as at the beginning and ending of a study. Love grows by giving itself away. If your circle becomes too large for easy face-to-face conversations, you can simply form a second discussion circle in another room in your home.

Surrendering

God is most pleased by a heart that is fully his. Each group session will provide group members a chance to surrender their hearts to God in prayer and worship. Group prayer requests and prayer time should be included every week.

18. This question is meant to encourage quiet time at home each day throughout the week. Here you can help the group see the importance of making time with God a priority. Read through this section and be prepared to help the group understand how important it is to fill our minds with the Word of God. If people already have a good Bible reading plan and commitment, that is great, but you may have people who struggle to stay in the Word daily. Sometimes beginning with a simple commitment to a short daily reading can start a habit that changes their life. The *Reflections* pages at the end of each session include verses that were either talked about in the session or support

the teaching of the session. They are very short readings with a few lines to encourage people to write down their thoughts. Remind the group about these *Reflections* each week after the *Surrendering* section. Encourage the group to commit to a next step in prayer, Bible reading, or meditation on the Word.

19. As you move to a time of sharing prayer requests, be sure to remind the group of the importance of confidentiality and keeping what is shared in the group within the group. Everyone must feel that the personal things they share will be kept in confidence if you are to have safety and bonding among group members.

    Use the *Prayer and Praise Report* in the *Appendix* to record your prayer requests. There you can keep track of requests and celebrate answers to prayer.

Session Two   The Pharisee and the Tax Collector

Growing

3. The people who were confident of their own righteousness and looked down on everybody else were the Pharisees and other religious leaders who saw themselves as the only ones righteous enough to be acceptable to God. Refer to the *Study Notes* in this session for more insight into the Pharisees. Such self-righteousness is damning (Rom. 10:3, Phil. 3:9) because we all fall short of God's standard (Matt. 5:48) and are in need of salvation. See Luke 15:16 and Romans 14:10 for additional insight into this verse.

4. The Pharisees were the most pious laypeople of the day, while the tax collectors were sharks. Yet both could approach God freely. We don't have to clean up before we approach God; we need to approach him for his forgiveness and help in cleaning up our act.

5. The Pharisee stood up and prayed about himself: The Pharisee's prayer is entirely about himself. See Matthew 6:5 and Luke 22:41 for additional insight into this verse.

    "God, I thank you that I . . ." The key word here is *that. Thank you that I* . . . reinforces Jesus's assertion in verse 9 that the Pharisees believed their righteousness was complete.

    "I am not like other men—robbers, evildoers, adulterers—or even like this tax collector." The Pharisee told God what a good man he was. He thanked God that he was not a sinner like everyone else. In this he erred in thinking that he was "not a sinner." He lacked humility before God. Thanking God for who he was reveals that the Pharisee gave God the credit for who he was, but he considered himself better than other people, using other people as his standard for measuring righteousness. God, however, uses himself as the standard for righteousness, and he views arrogance and lack of compassion as sins on the level of adultery and theft. See Romans 3:23.

"I fast twice a week and give a tenth of all I get." He was devout in his external observance but unaware that God cared about sins of the heart. See Luke 11:42 for additional insight.

The Pharisee was obsessed with himself. He despised the tax collector (and others)—literally counting them as nothing. The Pharisee's prayer lacked humility before God.

6. But the tax collector stood at a distance. The tax collector's behavior was noticeably humble; he stood back in an unassuming posture that highlighted his self-assessment of unworthiness. See Luke 22:41.

"He would not even look up to heaven": the tax collector appeared to know the extent of his sin. He didn't feel worthy to even lift his eyes to God. See Ezra 9:6 for additional insight.

". . . but beat his breast and said, 'God, have mercy on me, a sinner.'" He recognized himself as a sinner and had come to the one place where he knew he could find forgiveness. He humbly recognized that he did not deserve mercy, yet he petitioned God for mercy nonetheless. He beat his chest—a sign of sorrow—praying for God to be merciful to him. See Jeremiah 31:19 for additional insight.

7. The tax collector went home justified because he humbled himself, faced his sin, repented of his sin, and so could be forgiven. The Pharisee denied that he had sin, so he was unable to be forgiven. Without forgiveness of sin, a person is unjustified (has a broken relationship with God).

9. No one can do anything to deserve mercy, justification, or even salvation from God. Acceptance before God cannot be achieved by good deeds, piety, or any amount of self-proclaimed righteousness. Being humble requires having a true perspective about ourselves in relation to God. It's impossible to have a genuine relationship with God if we're lying to ourselves and God about our sins. It's impossible to turn away from a sin and toward God if we're too proud to admit it. God will help us break free from terrible sins, but he can't do so unless we choose humility. See Philippians 2:3 for additional insight.

10. Some things that may come to mind are that our prayers need to be honest, genuine, candid, and humble, or that confession is an important element of prayer. Many of us think our prayers need to sound good, but God doesn't want to be impressed.

Developing

11. Here is an opportunity for group members to consider where they can take a next step toward getting involved in ministering to the body of Christ in your local church. Encourage group members to use the *Personal Health Plan* to jot down their next step and plan how and when they will begin.

12. We encourage an outward focus for your group because groups that become too inwardly focused tend to become unhealthy over time. People naturally gravitate to feeding themselves through Bible study, prayer, and social time, so it's usually up to the leader to push them to consider how this inward nourishment can overflow into outward concern for others. Never forget: Jesus came to seek and save the lost and to find a shepherd for every sheep.

Session Three The Great Banquet

Connecting

2. It's time to start thinking about what your group will do when you're finished with this study. Now is the time to ask how many people will be joining you so you can choose a study and have the books available when you meet for the next session.

Growing

3. The context of the parable is a Middle Eastern banquet, a huge affair where guests of high social status have been invited and have accepted that invitation. The invited guests represent the nation of Israel, who, as God's special people, receive the first invitation. The invitation represents an offer of salvation.

4. Their excuses are much like the excuses people use today to delay accepting God's offer of salvation. They want to tend to business (new field, oxen) or their personal lives (getting married). The guests decide that other matters are more important.

6. In a shocking cultural turn, the master decides to invite the poor, the crippled, the blind, and the lame—yet the banquet hall is still not filled.
   No ancient wealthy person would ever invite the poor and handicapped. This surprising statement would have told Jesus's hearers that God's kingdom is for those whom society deems unacceptable.

7. God wants his house to be full. These guests possibly represent the Gentiles, all the other people of the world who will accept God's salvation. The Jews' rejection of Jesus was tragic, but God turned it to bring blessing to the Gentiles. And God isn't done with the Jews either (see Romans 9–11).

8. These outsiders included those who didn't take much effort to practice Judaism properly, those who couldn't financially afford to practice all the laws properly (most poor people), those who collaborated with the Romans and oppressed their fellow Jews, prostitutes, those in professions that made it hard to practice the Jewish purity customs (tanning leather, for example, meant contact with dead carcasses, which were ritually unclean), Samaritans, and other outsiders to whom Jesus ministered. The handicapped were

considered ritually unclean by some Jewish groups. The parable hints that the invitation will even go to the Gentiles, the ultimate outsiders.

9. None of those who refuse the invitation are admitted to the ultimate banquet—the messianic banquet. (See the *Study Notes* about the messianic banquet.) It's easy to feel smug about the Jews who rejected Jesus, but if we do that, we're as bad as the Pharisee in last week's parable who unwisely patted himself on the back. Instead we need to ask, "To what is God inviting me, and am I making excuses?"

Sharing

11. It is important to return to the *Circles of Life* and engage the group in identifying people who need to know Christ more deeply. Encourage a commitment to praying for God's guidance and an opportunity to share with each of them.

Surrendering

15. It is important each week to allow time for the group to share prayer requests and praises. This is likely the most important part of bonding your group and building deep relational connections. Encourage the group to keep a record of requests and praises on the *Prayer and Praise Report*. Reviewing ongoing requests and praises encourage the group as they recall God's faithfulness. Also continue to encourage your group to use the *Reflections* pages daily.

Session Four The Good Samaritan

Connecting

1. Whether your group is ending or continuing, it's important to celebrate where you have grown together. Take a few minutes for group members to share one thing they learned or a commitment they made or renewed during this study. They may also want to share what they enjoyed most about the study and about this group.

Growing

3. An expert in the Mosaic law would have known the answers to these questions according to the law and the tradition, so Jesus let him answer his own question in verses 25–26, then told a story that invited thought.

4. The law wasn't all picky little rules. It was God's law and so was good. Jesus wasn't opposed to the law. What infuriated the experts was that he

claimed to have authority to reject their interpretations and applications of the law in favor of his own.

5. The lawyer's question in verse 29 indicates that he didn't understand or possibly wanted to limit the law's demand and his responsibility. He may have been among those interpreters who held that only Jews qualified as neighbors one was required to love, but Jesus treated this command as far-reaching. Also, the lawyer should have recognized his inability to fulfill this command without help. Instead, he tried to justify himself, that is, to defend himself against the implications of Jesus's words.

6. Listeners would have understood the picture Jesus painted in verse 30. You could argue that he means them to think badly of these respected men because they don't help this stranger. Or you could argue that he means them to see these men as behaving the way most people in their position would. Either way, Jesus means to provoke his hearers to think about these respectable men's choice. Parables are meant to make us think.

7. The Samaritan took pity on him (v. 33). There is no indication that he even thought twice about what should be done. The Samaritan's actions show us that risky, sacrificial love is designed to be a lifestyle. We shouldn't ask, "Who am I obliged to love?" Instead we should ask, "What opportunities to love are around me?"

8. Love takes risks and makes sacrifices to help someone in need, regardless of racial and cultural tensions, or even the cost (v. 35). While loving as defined in the parable may seem impossible to live by, Jesus shows that this love that comes from God penetrates those barriers previously impenetrable.

9. We can look to Jesus's example. Have the group brainstorm some ways we can reach out to others as Jesus did. Allow people to just offer whatever ideas come to mind. Ask someone in the group to write these ideas down.

Sharing

11. Encourage group members to consider developing their salvation story as a tool for sharing their faith with others. Begin the process during your group time and encourage the group to complete the exercise at home. As leader, you should review the "Tips" section of *Telling Your Story* yourself in advance and be ready to share your ideas about this process with the group.

DEEPENING
LIFE TOGETHER SERIES

Deepening Life Together is a series of Bible studies that offers small groups an opportunity to explore biblical subjects in several categories: books of the Bible (*Acts, Romans, John, Ephesians, Revelation*), theology (*Promises of God, Parables*), and spiritual disciplines (*Prayers of Jesus*).

A *Deepening Life Together* Video Teaching DVD companion is available for each study in the series. For each study session, the DVD contains a lesson taught by a master teacher backed by scholars giving their perspective on the subject.

Every study includes activities based on five biblical purposes of the church: Connecting, Growing, Developing, Sharing, and Surrendering. These studies will help your group deepen your walk with God while you discover what he has created you for and how you can turn his desires into an everyday reality in your lives. Experience the transformation firsthand as you begin deepening your life together.